NUMBERS IN MOTION
SOPHIE KOWALEVSKI, QUEEN OF MATHEMATICS

BY LAURIE WALLMARK

ILLUSTRATED BY YEVGENIA NAYBERG

Creston Books

Sophie carefully pulled the string, and the top spun across her desk.
She watched the toy as it wibbled and wobbled, tilting this way and that.

It didn't spin in a circle.

And it didn't move in a spiral.

The top slowed...

and slowed...

and toppled over.

This wasn't a game for Sophie. It was work. Even though she was a mathematics professor, Sophie hadn't been able to figure out the equations to describe the top's rotation. But she kept trying. If she succeeded, her math might help scientists calculate the path of planets and design faster ships.

Many mathematicians had tried to find equations that explained the complex movements of a spinning top — big or small, narrow or wide, wooden or clay — but none had yet succeeded. Could Sophie?

$$T^2 = \frac{4\pi^2 r^3}{GM}$$

As a young girl, Sophie paid little attention to the toys scattered about her bedroom. Instead, she spent hours staring at pages and pages of math problems covering her walls from floor to ceiling. When her father had run out of wallpaper for their new home, he had pasted his old college math notes on her walls instead.

With her finger, Sophie traced the mysterious numbers and symbols, searching for patterns. She was fascinated by the secret language of calculus. Although she couldn't yet understand it, that didn't matter. It was as if the concepts were entering through her fingertips, travelling up her arm, and finding a home deep inside her brain.

As she got older, Sophie's interest in math kept growing. When she was a teenager, a neighbor loaned her father a physics textbook he had written. Sophie begged and begged her father to let her read the professor's book. Finally, he gave in.

The math in the book was difficult, but Sophie was up for the challenge. Line by line, page by page, she worked out the math and physics formulas. That is, until she got to the chapter on optics, the behavior of light.

To master this subject, Sophie needed to understand trigonometry, the mathematics of triangles. Unfortunately, she hadn't gotten that far in her studies.

Sophie didn't let that stop her. Instead of using trigonometry, she worked out an alternate approach with math she did know. She could substitute a line, called a chord, which connects two points on a circle. Sophie didn't know that before trigonometry was invented, mathematicians had used this same method.

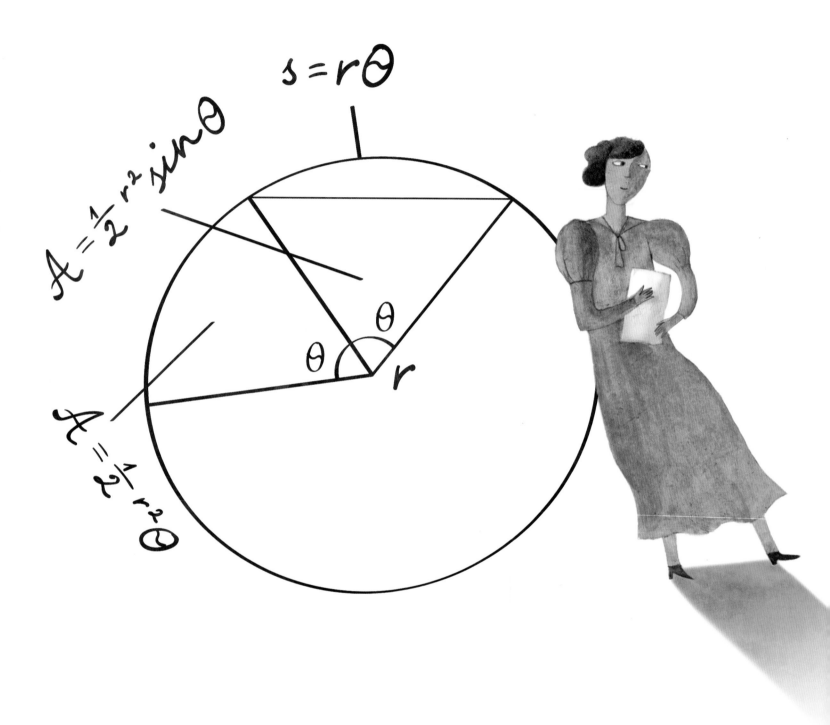

Sophie showed her work to the professor who had written the book. Impressed, the physicist urged Sophie's father to let her study more advanced mathematics. Such extraordinary talents should be developed, not wasted. Sophie's father agreed and hired a mathematician to teach his teenage daughter.

The tutor helped, but he could only take Sophie so far. To continue her studies at a higher level, she wanted to go to Heidelberg University in Germany. But in order to leave Russia, she needed a passport. And to get a passport, she needed the permission of her father or her husband.

Her father wouldn't give his approval, so Sophie looked for a man who would agree to be her partner in a marriage of convenience. She found a student, Vladimir Kovalevski, who also wanted to study abroad. Vladimir agreed to this fake marriage, and together they left for Germany. Once there, they led separate lives, sometimes not even living together.

When Sophie went to enroll at the university, she discovered they didn't allow women students. She went from professor to professor, trying to convince them she deserved a place in their classes. After looking at her impressive work, they all decided to let Sophie attend their lectures, but not as an official student. She couldn't receive college credit for these classes.She wouldn't get a degree.

$$\nabla^2 u_3 = \frac{\partial^2 u_3}{\partial x^2} + \frac{\partial^2 u_3}{\partial y^2} = 0$$

$$\frac{\partial^2}{\partial x^2}(h(x)\,\wp(y)) +$$

$$\wp(y)\frac{d^2 h}{dx^2} + h$$

$$\frac{1}{h}\frac{d^2 h}{dx^2} = -\frac{1}{\wp}\frac{\partial^2 \wp}{\partial y^2} = -$$

$$\lambda_n =$$

As the only woman in her classes, Sophie rarely spoke up. One day, while the professor was lecturing, she spotted a mistake on the blackboard. With a pounding heart, she walked to the front of the room.

The other students gaped at this girl who dared to interrupt the lecture. Sophie picked up a piece of chalk, corrected the error, and silently returned to her seat. The professor continued speaking as if nothing had happened.

After Sophie had taken all the math classes she could at Heidelberg, she moved to Berlin, the European center of mathematical research. But the University of Berlin in 1870 was even more rigidly opposed to women taking classes. They didn't even allow women to set foot on campus. Her only choice was to study privately.

Sophie approached Karl Weierstrass, a leading mathematician at the university. Before he would consider working with her, Weierstrass gave her the same math exam he used with his advanced students.

Weierstrass expected her to fail, but when he looked over her finished exam, a smile stretched across his face. Sophie had gotten all the problems right.

For the next four years, Weierstrass repeated all of his lectures a second time, just for Sophie. Day after day, she studied, often sixteen hours at a time or more. Before long, Sophie was Weierstrass's star student.

Now Sophie had the chance to receive a doctoral degree, but she needed to be the first person to solve a complex math problem.

She chose a topic in Partial Differential Equations (PDEs). These are mathematical tools that can be used to describe many natural phenomena, such as sound, heat, and movement. Tools like these could help Sophie solve the spinning top problem.

After much hard work, Sophie solved the equations she was working on. Soon she would achieve her dream. She would become Dr. Sophie Kowalevski.

Except, another mathematician had been working on a similar problem. Before Sophie had a chance to submit her proof, his paper was accepted for publication. He was first. Sophie was second.

She had to start all over again.

This time, Sophie wasn't taking any chances. She decided to work on not one, but three mathematical problems. Publishing one thesis was an incredible accomplishment, but to do three was almost unheard of.

In her first paper, Sophie used math to investigate the complicated shape of Saturn's rings. She determined the cross-section of the rings must be an oval, not an ellipse, as previously thought. This finding led to her nickname, the "Muse of Heavens."

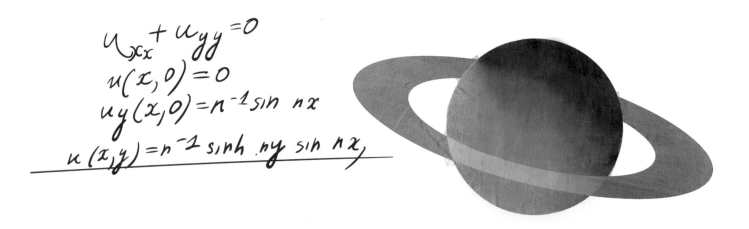

$$u_{xx} + u_{yy} = 0$$
$$u(x,0) = 0$$
$$u_y(x,0) = n^{-1} \sin nx$$
$$u(x,y) = n^{-1} \sinh ny \sin nx,$$

Next, she analyzed a topic in pure mathematics. These are concepts that aren't used in the real world...yet. An example is imaginary numbers. When first discovered, they were only used in pure mathematics. Now they have real-life applications in fields like wireless technology.

Cauchy Kowalevski Theorem

$$G(z$$

$$\frac{C_r}{r-z}$$

$$\partial_t^j h(x,0) =$$

$$u_1(t) = \sum_{n=0}^{\infty} \frac{t^n}{n!} \left(\partial z^n \right)$$

$$d_t^i = F\left(x, t, \partial_t^j \partial_x^{\alpha} h \right)$$

$$\sum_{n=0}^{\infty} a_n \sum_{j=0}^{n}$$

$$G(y) = \int_0^x \frac{1}{F(x)}$$

$$u(x) \sim \sum \frac{1}{a!} D$$

$$f(z) = \sum_{j=0}^{\infty} \left(\sum_{n=j}^{\infty} \binom{n}{j} a_n (d-c)^{n-j} \right) (z-d)^j$$

For her third paper, Sophie started with the findings of another mathematician, Augustin-Louis Cauchy. Building on his work, she proved a major finding about the general theory of Partial Differential Equations. Her discovery was so important that mathematicians named it the Cauchy-Kowalevski Theorem.

Still, the University of Berlin refused to give Sophie a degree. They thought only men should receive doctorates. Not women, no matter how brilliant.

Sophie was not about to give up. She found a different school, Göttingen University, willing to grant her a degree based on her exceptional work. Sophie earned her doctorate in mathematics with the highest distinction.

Degree in hand, it was time for Sophie to find a teaching job. Only one school was willing to hire her, Stockholm University in Sweden. They offered her a position as lecturer in mathematics. Because she was a woman, she had to work for no pay.

Sophie took the job. It was a start.

When Sophie entered the classroom for her first lecture, her twelve students, all men, stood and applauded. She was such a good teacher that at the end of her first semester, Stockholm University promoted her to staff professor and at last granted her a salary. Sophie was the first woman to become a full professor at a university in Northern Europe.

The local townspeople greatly admired their new neighbor. They referred to her as "our Professor Sophie." Word of this brilliant woman, the "Queen of Mathematics," spread across Europe.

Looking for a new area of math to research, Sophie returned to one that she had tried, and failed, to solve before — how to describe the unpredictable motion of a spinning top. Through the years, her work had led her to other areas of math, but she always came back to this one.

In 1888, the Paris Academy of Science offered an important award, the Bordin Prize, for anyone who could solve the spinning-top problem. Only the very best mathematicians had a chance of winning the competition.

Day and night, Sophie worked on the many difficult equations. Numbers and symbols filled her head, at first a jumble, then falling into patterns. Whenever she reached a dead end in her thinking, she figured out another approach. Step-by-step, she arranged all the mathematical bits and pieces into place. And there it was.

Sophie had her solution.

$$c_2 = L_1 y_1 + L_2 y_2 + L$$

It was time to submit her work. She wrote fifty mathematics-filled pages to explain how she solved the problem. Her analysis, now known as the Kowalevski Property, has yet to be improved upon.

Sophie also included her personal motto in her submission, "Say what you know, do what you must, come what may." She did not, though, sign her name, since the contest was anonymous. That way no one would know her work was by a woman.

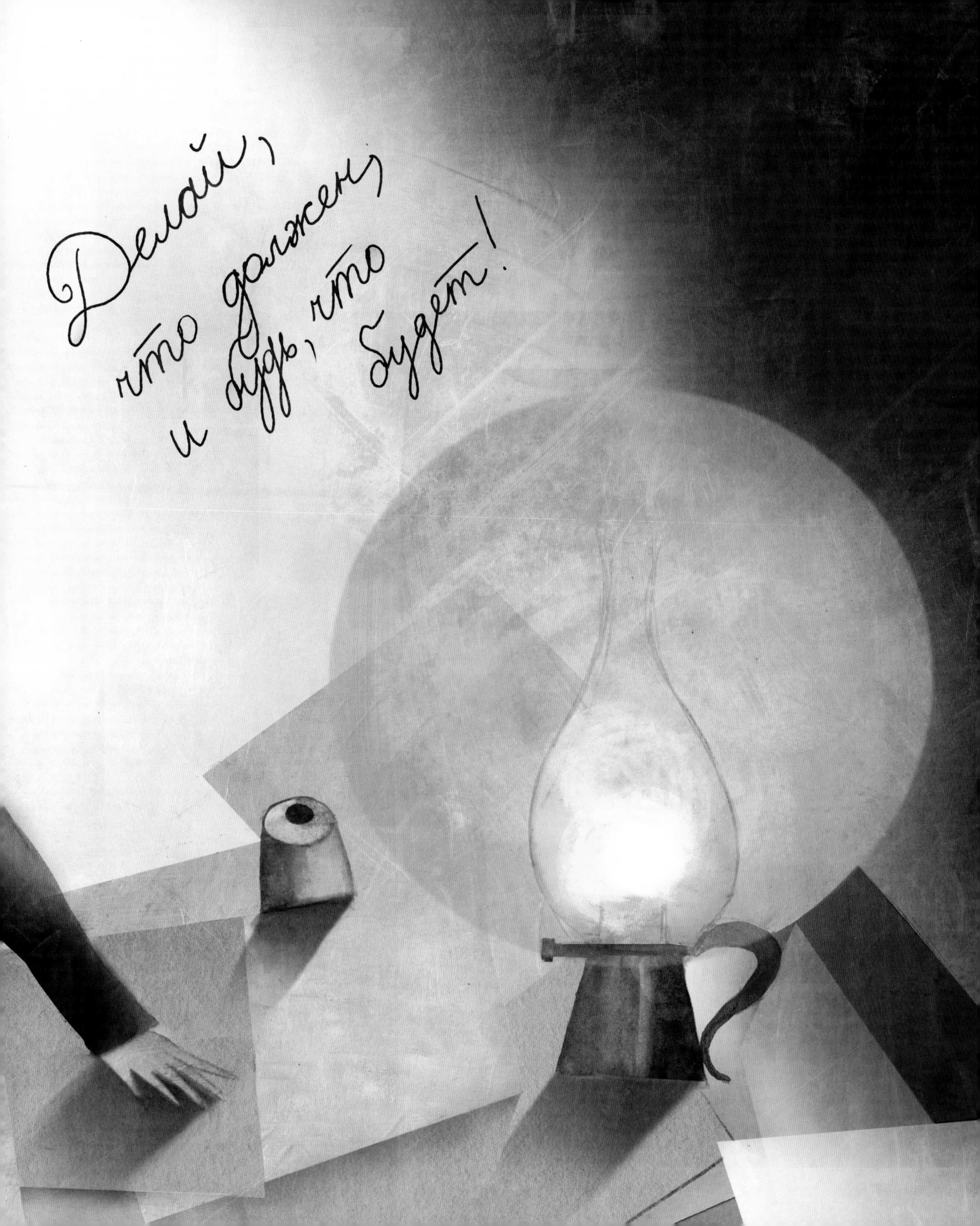
Делай,
что должен,
и будь, что
будет!

The Academy reviewed the submissions and declared all the answers incomplete or incorrect. Until they reached Sophie's paper. Her solution was perfect, both clear and elegant. Recognizing the importance of her work, they increased the award from 3,000 to 5,000 francs.

Sophie had always known that women plus math added up to a powerful equation.

Now the rest of the world knew it, too.

AUTHOR'S NOTE

Sophie's many "firsts" made her a role model for women in math and science. She was the first woman to receive a doctorate in mathematics that required original research, the first to hold a university chair in mathematics, the first to be elected to the Russian Imperial Academy of Sciences, and the first to be the editor of a major scientific journal.

But Sophie was more than a brilliant mathematician. She was also a talented writer. Through the years, the little girl who wrote poetry behind her nanny's back never forgot her love of writing. While teaching and doing mathematical research, Sophie still found the time to write a memoir, novel, short stories, newspaper articles, two plays, and hundreds of poems.

Her most famous work, *Nihilist Girl,* is a novel about a young aristocratic woman who wants to devote her life to social justice. Through this story, Sophie made the argument that women should have the same opportunities and freedoms as men. A similar theme ran through her memoir, *A Russian Childhood.* Here, Sophie detailed how she wanted more in life than to be a wife and mother.

Sophie's marriage to Vladimir was initially a marriage of convenience, a way for her to leave Russia and study mathematics. During most of her time in Germany, she and her husband did not share a home. But after Sophie received her doctorate, the two returned to Russia and lived together as man and wife. There, she gave birth to her only child, a daughter, Sofya, nicknamed Fufa. When Fufa was two years old, Sophie left Vladimir for good and moved with her daughter to Berlin.

After Vladimir died, Sophie fell in love with Maxim Kovalevski, a distant cousin of his. Maxim proposed marriage, but he insisted on one condition — Sophie must give up her beloved mathematics. Sophie rejected his proposal. Stop doing mathematics? Never!

Sophie was the first woman to be a professional mathematician since Hypatia in fifth century Egypt. Her fellow mathematicians didn't care that she was a woman. They knew Sophie's work was equal to that of any mathematician of her time. Sophie published ten papers in mathematics and mechanics, the branch of physics having to do with the study of motion. The methods she discovered have increasing application to mathematical physics today.

Sophie's exceptional talent for creative thinking was the fuel that powered her notable accomplishments in both writing and mathematics. Understanding the similarity between the two fields, she said, "The poet must see more deeply than other people, and the mathematician must do the same."

SOPHIE'S MATH

Although Sophie Kowalevski made contributions in many areas of mathematics, she is most well known for solving the mathematical mermaid problem. It was called this because mathematicians thought the chance of finding the solution was as likely as the chance of seeing a mermaid.

But what exactly is this puzzler? It's more officially known as the solid body rotation problem. In other words, how do you describe the motion of a spinning object using mathematical equations? This object can be anything from a small child's top to a giant faraway planet.

It sounds easy enough, doesn't it? Picture what happens when you spin a top. If you look at the top from above, the pointy end stays in one place and the body goes around and around in a circle. Mathematicians have long known the basic equation to describe the path of circle. It's

$$x^2 + y^2 = r^2 .$$

Problem solved.

But what if the top is slightly off-center when you spin it? Or your fingers twitch at the last minute? What happens then? What equations describe your top's seemingly random wobbles across the table?

That's where the more complicated mathematics come in. Sophie used a technique called Partial Differential Equations (PDEs). A PDE defines the rules about how something changes. Its solution is a function that matches any numerical input to the correct output. These types of equations can be difficult to solve. A clever mathematician like Sophie has to figure out a function that follows all the rules — no exceptions.

PDEs are used extensively in applied mathematics to represent real-world phenomena. Scientists and mathematicians use PDEs in many fields, such as physics, biology, medicine, and engineering. These equations can describe anything from ocean waves to how a robot walks, from a beating heart to fireplace flames.

But why was it so important for Sophie to solve the solid body rotation problem? What was the big deal? Here are a few examples of how her solution helps us today.

There's a new, scary ride at the amusement park. You and the rest of the riders take your places around the edge of a large, circular platform. The safety bars drop down, and the ride begins. The platform rotates faster and faster. Then, a long metal arm swings the riders and the platform high up into the sky. Round and round you go. Aren't you glad the engineers who designed the ride used Sophie's mathematics to make sure your ride is safe...and fun?

While at the park, you hear an announcement about a robot demonstration. You and your friends hurry over to watch. You're amazed to see how well the robot walks and even climbs stairs. But when it extends its giant hand toward a glass of water, you and your friends shake your heads. There's no way that robot will be able to pick up the glass without knocking it over.

Good thing the robot's creators knew about Sophie's work. At the last minute it rotates its fingers around its wrist so they line up correctly with the glass. The robot picks it up without spilling a single drop.

And now for an example that's important for all of us. You may have read that a giant asteroid struck the Earth many millions of years ago and most likely wiped out all the dinosaurs. What about the next time a monster asteroid, following an unknown route, wanders near the Earth? Will it hit our planet or will it pass us by? Using Sophie's solution, astrophysicists can predict the asteroid's path. This could give us enough warning to avoid catastrophe.

All thanks to Sophie.

TIMELINE

January 15, 1850	Sofia Vasilyevna Korvin-Krukovskaya is born
September 27, 1868	Marries Vladimir Kowalevsky
1869 - 1870	Studies at Heidelberg University
1870 - 1874	Studies in Berlin with Prof. Karl Weierstrass
August 29, 1874	Receives Ph.D. from Göttingen University (first woman to receive a doctorate in math that required original research)
October 17, 1878	Daughter Sofya ("Fufa") Vladimirovna is born
September 1883	Receives offer as a lecturer at Stockholm University
June 28, 1884	Appointed Professor of Mathematics for five years at Stockholm University
December 24, 1888	Awarded the Bordin Prize
June, 1889	Receives lifetime appointment at Stockholm University (first woman in modern times to hold a university chair)
February 10, 1891	Sophie Kowalevski dies of pneumonia

SELECTED BIBLIOGRAPHY

Audin, Michèle. *Remembering Sofya Kovalevskaya*. London: Springer, 2011.

Kennedy, Don H. *Little Sparrow: A Portrait of Sophia Kovalevsky*. Athens: Ohio U Press, 1983.

Kochina, Pelageya. *Love and Mathematics: Sofya Kovalevskaya*. Trans. Michael Burov. Moscow: Mir Publishers, 1985.

Koblitz, Ann Hibner. *A Convergence of Lives: Sofia Kovalevskaia: Scientist, Writer, Revolutionary*. Boston: Birkhäuser, 1993.

Kovalevskaja, Sofya V. *A Russian Childhood*. Trans. Beatrice Stillman. New York: Springer, 1978.

Spicci, Joan. *Beyond the Limit: The Dream of Sofya Kovalevskaya*. New York: Forge, 2002.